This is a Forest

Gina Zorzi & Trace Taylor

This is a forest. Forests have trees.

Forests have lots of

Forests have trees that look like this.

Forests have been the king

Water

Trees like lots of water.

Stream

River

They get water from streams and rivers.

8

Pond

Lake

Shelter

Robin

Many animals live in the forest.

Raccoon

Wild Boar

Some live under the trees.

Gopher

Food

White-tailed Deer

Animals eat trees.

Green Parrot

Animals eat the flowers from trees.

15

White-tailed Deer

They eat the leaves.

Starling

They eat the fruit.

Herbivores

Moose

Squirrel

Rabbit

Beaver

All of these animals eat plants.

Carnivores

Gray Tree Frog

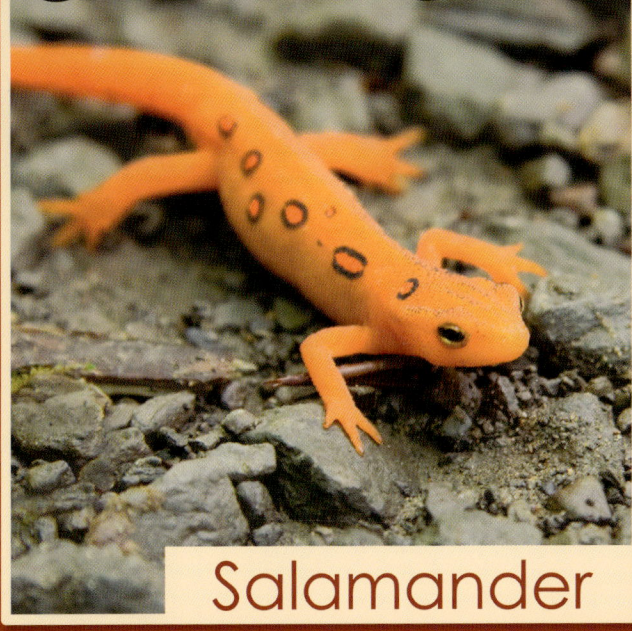
Salamander

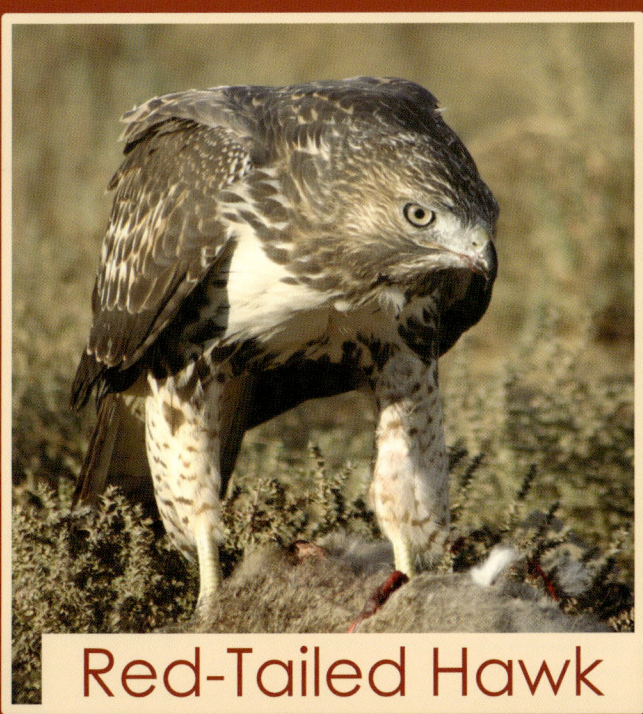
Red-Tailed Hawk

Timber Rattlesnake

All of these animals eat animals.

19

Omnivores

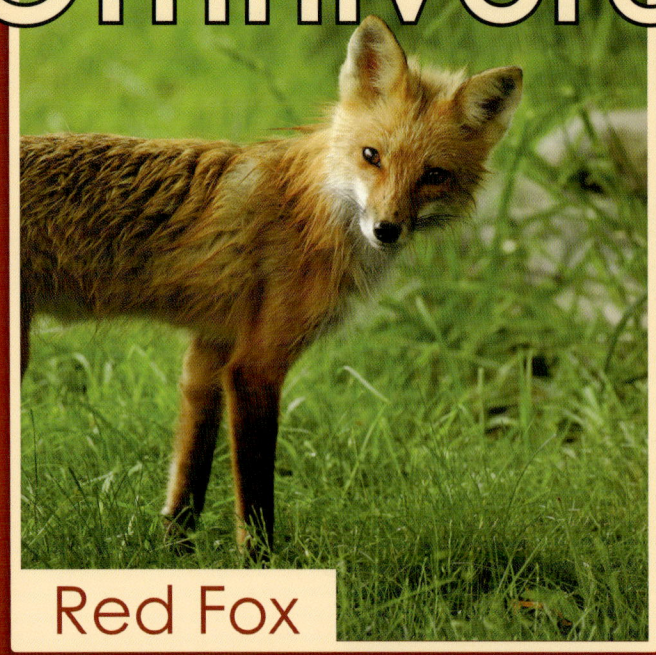
Red Fox

Timber Wolf

Skunk

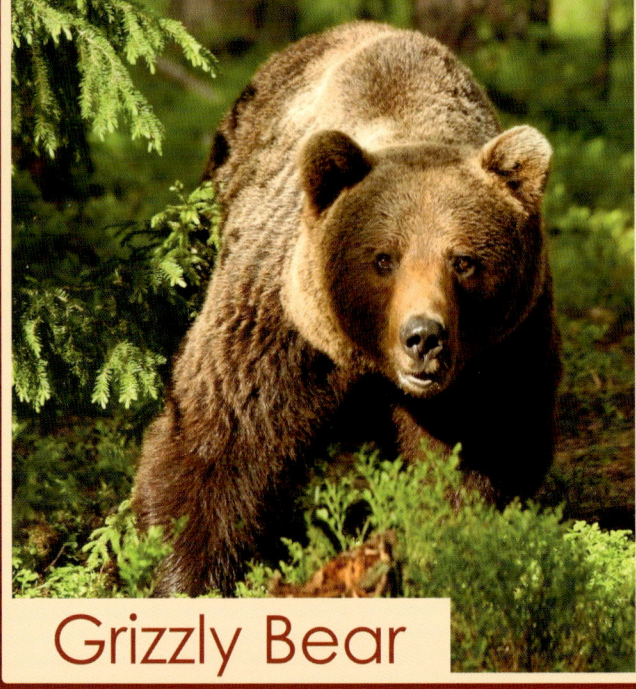
Grizzly Bear

All of these animals eat animals and plants.

Camouflage

Grizzly Bear

Forest animals look like the forest.

Timber Wolf

This animal looks like the forest.

22

People

People live in the forest.

23

People make houses from trees.

People make all of these from trees.

25

Forest Food Web

Water Cycle

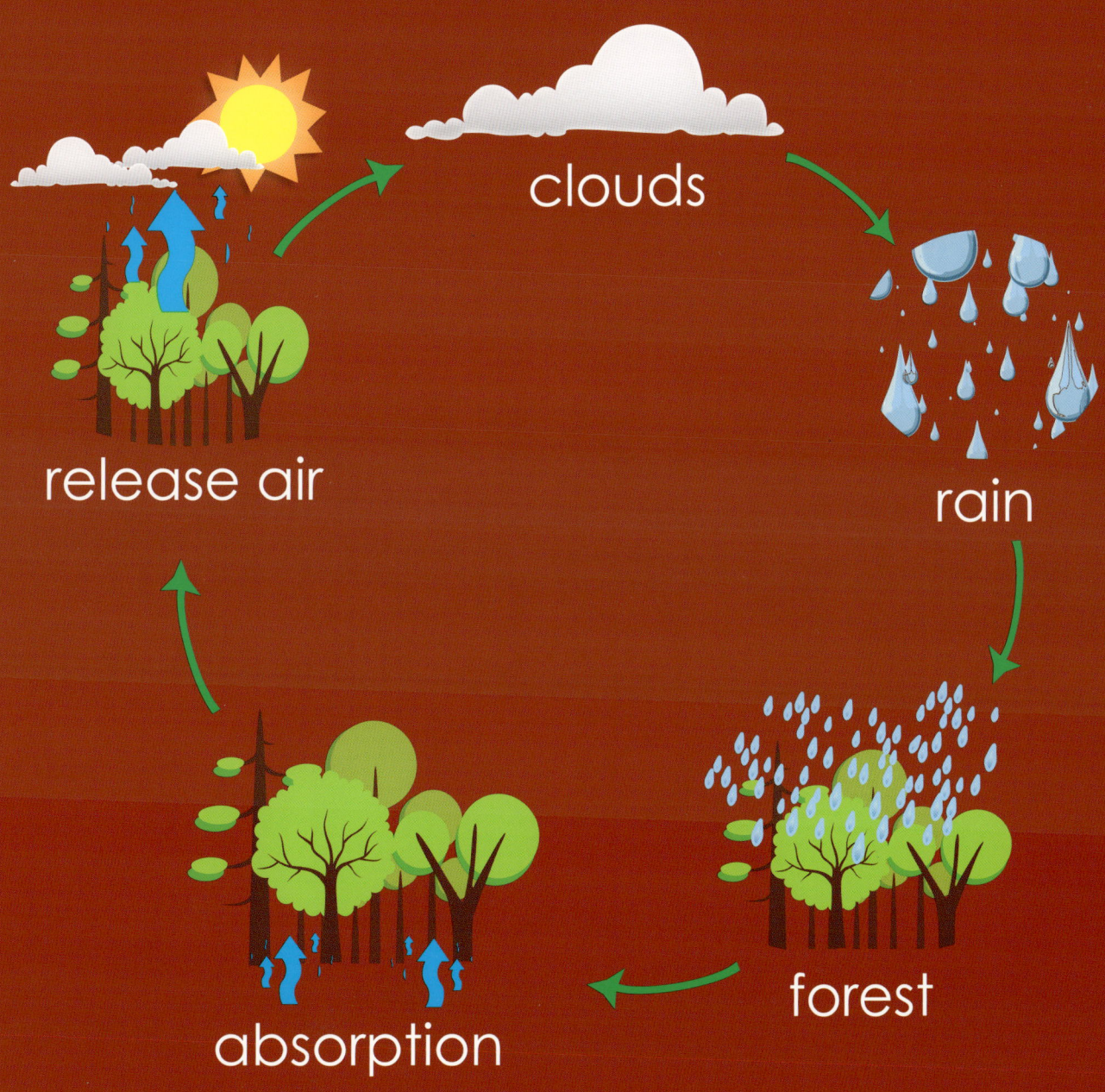

Power Words
How many can you read?

animal	eat	from	inside
make	many	these	under

Ecosystem Words

flowers	forest	fruit	ground	lakes
leaves	people	plants	ponds	rain
rivers	snow	streams	trees	water